ONE DIRECTION

POPULAR BOY BAND

KATIE LAJINESS

Big Buddy Books

An Imprint of Abdo Publishing
abdopublishing.com

BIG BUDDY **POP** BIOGRAPHIES

abdopublishing.com

Published by Abdo Publishing, a division of ABDO, PO Box 398166, Minneapolis, Minnesota 55439.
Copyright © 2016 by Abdo Consulting Group, Inc. International copyrights reserved in all countries.
No part of this book may be reproduced in any form without written permission from the publisher.
Big Buddy Books™ is a trademark and logo of Abdo Publishing.

Printed in the United States of America, North Mankato, Minnesota.
102015
012016

Cover Photo: Jon Kopaloff/Getty Images.
Interior Photos: © ACE/INFphoto.com/Corbis (p. 19); Associated Press (pp. 9, 13, 17, 21, 29);
Juan Naharro Gimenez/Getty Images (p. 5); Jean Nelson/Deposit Photos (p. 15);
Christopher Polk/Getty Images (p. 11); Charles Sykes/Invision/AP (pp. 15, 23, 25);
Stuart C. Wilson/Getty Images (p. 27); Kevin Winter/BMA2015/Getty Images (p. 31).

Coordinating Series Editor: Tamara L. Britton
Contributing Editor: Marcia Zappa
Graphic Design: Jenny Christensen

Library of Congress Cataloging-in-Publication Data

Lajiness, Katie, 1983- author.
 One Direction / Katie Lajiness.
     pages cm. -- (Big buddy pop biographies)
 Includes index.
 ISBN 978-1-68078-056-7
1. One Direction (Musical group)--Juvenile literature. 2. Rock musicians--England--Biography--
    Juvenile literature. I. Title.
 ML3930.O66L35 2016
 782.42164092'2--dc23
 [B]
                              2015034226

CONTENTS

RISING STARS

One Direction is a popular music group. The original members were Niall Horan, Zayn Malik, Liam Payne, Harry Styles, and Louis Tomlinson. Fans around the world love the band's songs.

SNAPSHOT

NAME (*left to right*):

Niall James Horan
Zain "Zayn" Javadd Malik
Louis William Tomlinson
Harry Edward Styles
Liam James Payne

BIRTHDAY:

September 13, 1993
January 12, 1993
December 24, 1991
February 1, 1994
August 29, 1993

ALBUMS:

Up All Night, Take Me Home,
Midnight Memories, Four, Made in the A.M.

STARTING OUT

One Direction formed in London, England, in 2010. Its members started out as **solo** artists on the British television talent show *The X Factor*. But, the show's judges thought the guys would be better as a boy band.

So, the boys formed One Direction. It took third place on *The X Factor*. Soon after, judge Simon Cowell asked the band to record an album.

WHERE IN THE WORLD?

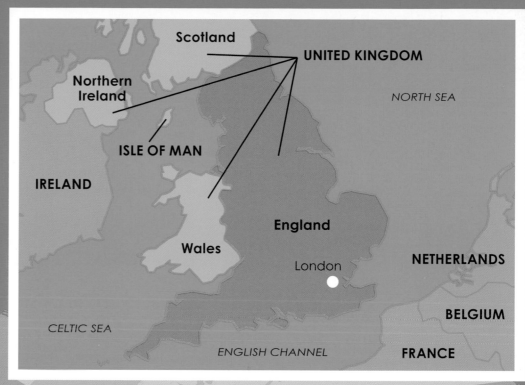

Scotland

Northern
Ireland

ISLE OF MAN

IRELAND

UNITED KINGDOM

NORTH SEA

England

Wales

London

NETHERLANDS

BELGIUM

CELTIC SEA

ENGLISH CHANNEL

FRANCE

N
W E
S

BIG BREAK

In 2011, One Direction **released** its first album, *Up All Night*. The band became a big hit in the United Kingdom! The album had popular songs such as "What Makes You Beautiful," "Gotta Be You," and "One Thing."

One Direction (*above*) received great advice from judge Simon Cowell (*right*). He is known for helping make successful music. Simon helped One Direction to sing well together.

Many people follow One Direction on the Internet. The band's fans are very active on **social media**.

Fans around the world use social media to share photos and videos of One Direction. And, the band uses it to send messages to fans. The group's popularity continues to spread throughout the world.

In 2012, One Direction sang at the MTV Video Music Awards. They sang "One Thing," and the crowd went wild!

In 2012, One Direction's second album came out. *Take Me Home* sold 540,000 copies in its first week! The following year, the band **released** *Midnight Memories*. This was the world's best-selling album of 2013!

In 2014, the band released *Four*. One Direction became the first band to have its first four albums **debut** at number one on the charts!

DID YOU KNOW ?

The band members are authors! They wrote *One Direction: Forever Young: Our Official X Factor Story* and *Dare to Dream: Life as One Direction.*

The boys of One Direction are a big hit with young fans. They are greeted by screaming young girls wherever they go!

IRISH EYES

Niall James Horan was born in Mullingar, Ireland, on September 13, 1993. His parents are Bobby Horan and Maura Gallagher. Niall has an older brother.

As a child, Niall loved music. When he was about 12, Niall learned to play the **guitar**. He was also in the school **choir**.

Niall is the group's only Irish member. He speaks with an Irish accent.

THE QUIET ONE

Zain "Zayn" Javadd Malik was born in Bradford, England, on January 12, 1993. His parents are Yaser and Patricia Malik. Zayn has three sisters.

In 2015, Zayn decided to leave One Direction. The band continued with just four members.

DID YOU KNOW?
Zayn is part Irish, English, and Pakistani.

Zayn has many tattoos. He has his grandfather's name tattooed on his chest.

BIG VOICE

Liam James Payne was born in Wolverhampton, England, on August 29, 1993. His parents are Geoff and Karen Payne. He has two older sisters.

Growing up, Liam loved singing and dancing. At age 16, he **auditioned** for *The X Factor* a second time. This time, he sang the Justin Timberlake song "Cry Me a River." And, the judges loved Liam's voice!

Liam enjoys songwriting. He helps write many of the band's songs.

THE FUNNY ONE

Harry Edward Styles was born in Worcestershire, England, on February 1, 1994. His parents are Desmond Styles and Anne Cox. Harry has an older sister.

In high school, Harry formed a band with friends. But, he never guessed he'd be part of a world-famous boy band!

Harry came up with the band's name.

WILD CARD

Louis William Tomlinson was born in Doncaster, England, on December 24, 1991. His parents are Troy Austin and Johannah Tomlinson.

In 2009, Louis tried out for *The X Factor*. He did not make it. But, Louis **auditioned** again in 2010. This time, he made it!

DID YOU KNOW

As a teenager, Louis did some acting on television.

Louis loves to shop! He is known for his great fashion sense.

SUPERSTARS

The guys of One Direction are very busy. When they are not on tour or recording albums, they are winning **awards**! As of 2015, the band has won five BRIT Awards and four MTV Video Music Awards, among others.

One Direction continues to grow in popularity. In 2014, *Billboard* named One Direction Artist of the Year.

In 2013, One Direction sang "Best Song Ever" at the MTV Video Music Awards.

Members of One Direction love to use their superstar **status** for worthy causes. The guys give their time to benefits for sick children and poor people around the world.

One Direction works with Rays of Sunshine, a benefit for sick children.

BUZZ

One Direction remains a popular band. For much of 2015, the band was on its fourth concert tour.

In 2015, One Direction **released** *Made in the A.M.* Then the band will be taking a break. Fans are excited to see what One Direction does next!

One Direction rocked its first show without Zayn. The crowd in South Africa was so excited to see the band's four members.

GLOSSARY

audition (aw-DIH-shuhn) to give a trial performance showcasing personal talent as a musician, a singer, a dancer, or an actor.

award something that is given in recognition of good work or a good act.

choir (KWEYE-uhr) a group of singers that perform together, usually in a church or school.

debut (DAY-byoo) to make a first appearance.

guitar (guh-TAHR) a stringed musical instrument played by strumming.

release to make available to the public.

social media a form of communication on the Internet where people can share information, messages, and videos. It may include blogs and online groups.

solo a performance by a single person.

status position or rank of a person or thing.

WEBSITES

To learn more about Pop Biographies, visit **booklinks.abdopublishing.com**.
These links are routinely monitored and updated to provide
the most current information available.

INDEX